Shadows Like These

Shadows Like These

Poems
by
Marilyn Taylor

Wm Caxton Ltd
Ellison Bay, Wisconsin
1994

Published by

Wm Caxton Ltd
12037 Highway 42
Ellison Bay, WI 54210

(414) 854-2955

Printed in the United States of America.

10   9   8   7   6   5   4   3   2   1

Library of Congress Cataloging-in-Publication Data

Taylor, Marilyn, 1939-
    Shadows like these : poems / by Marilyn Taylor.
        p.   cm.
    ISBN 0-940473-27-5 (alk. paper) : $12.50
    I. Title.
PS3570.A94515S53 1994
811'.54--dc20   94-26827
                                                                           CIP

ISBN# 0-940473-27-5

        This book is set in a version of Palatino type chosen for its
readability and attractiveness; it is printed on acid-neutral paper bound
in sewn signatures and is intended to provide a very long useful life.

Acknowledgements

Some of the poems in this volume were first published individually elsewhere. Acknowledgement and thanks is hereby given to the publishers and editors of the following magazines and anthologies for first publication of the poems listed:

Magazines & Journals:

Poetry: "To a Young Diver"; "Golden Warriors End Year With Big Loss"
Transactions: "Tercets from the Train"; "Miss Martin at Four O'Clock"
Poetry Northwest: "The Tenth Avenue Care Home"; "Late in the Wet Season"
Blue Unicorn: "A Love Song, Continued"
Indiana Review: "The Lovers at Eighty"; "Drive All Night"
Midland Review: "From the Ice Cave"
Kansas Quarterly: "The Globetrotter"
Plains Poetry Journal: "Sixty-Five"
Kalliope: "I Know a Bank Where the Wild Thyme Blows"
Midcoaster: "In Tanzania"
The Cream City Review: "Earth Mother"; "The Clown"
Poet Lore: "What They Don't Know"
Poets On: "Last Favor"
Wisconsin Review: "Speak to Me in the Oldest Tongue"

Anthologies:

Wisconsin Poets: "The Boy on the Plane"
Troika I (Thorntree Press): "The Showdown"; "Daisy Lane Gothic"; "Lady Hamilton's Portrait"; "No Two Exactly Alike"; "Piano Overture"; "Notice from the Sweet Chariot Funeral Parlor"; "The Vow"; "The Odalisques"
The Southern California Anthology: "Outside the Frame: The Photographer's Last Letters to Her Son"

Special thanks to Diane Knox for the art used on the dustjacket, cover, and title page.

Table of Contents

Interludes

Memorabilia

Eventualities

Affinities

The Lovers at Eighty

Fluted light from the window finds her
sleepless in the double bed, her eyes

measuring the chevron angle his knees make
under the coverlet. She is trying to recall

the last time they made love. It must have been
in shadows like these, the morning his hands

took their final tour along her shoulders and down
over the pearls of her vertebrae

to the cool dunes of her hips, his fingers
executing solemn little figures

of farewell. Strange — it's not so much
the long engagement as the disengagement

of their bodies that fills the hollow
curve of memory behind her eyes —

how the moist, lovestrung delicacy
with which they let each other go

had made a sound like taffeta
while decades flowed across them like a veil.

To a Young Diver

So long, silversides.
The lips of the sea
close over you.

I watch you shimmer
and vanish into
the inverted garden

where minnows flock
like sparrows
and tiny pods of air

sequin the powdered
shoulders of
the reef.

Deeper: obsidian walls
flicker with mystery —
fish are flame, coral sways

to the throb of
the young planet
in its skin.

Down there
you are only a fold
in the water, a mote

in time — yesterday spreads
beneath you, silent
as bedrock

while the future presses
upward: a helix rising
through pre-Cambrian blue

brightening
to gem turquoise
as you break the surface

streaming gold, festooned
with your tangled cargo,
your frieze of stars.

On Marrying Well

Observe this retinue of towheads
she has taken for her own,
this cotillion of a family —

not the dark and the hairy-armed
with blunt tongues flapping,
but a flock of finches

whose berries, figs and apricots
leave no room at table for
dense black bread

nor for children, sweating
and speechless around chunks of chocolate
liquefying in their cheeks.

Instead, the room fills up
with upholstered syllables : *Armani.*
Vichyssoise. Eleuthera.

Laughter chimes — jewelled bracelets dropping
on parquet. Conversation shifty — intricate
as chess, or rare Bordeaux.

No third helpings here. No undershirts,
armpits, toothpicks, saxophones
or feet on the table.

The wine is thin, and
full of water.

Daisy Lane Gothic

This is a suburb; not the sort of place
where ruins are the norm. But there it was,
behind the thickets in the vacant lot:
a gate. And just behind the gate, a strip
of cinders — the ghost of what had been a wall.

The man, the dog, and I were mystified —
had there once been a cottage here, then
a fire? How long ago, and of what melodrama
was this scorched rectangle the final scene?
We scrabbled in our mental underbrush

and came up with a fragile heroine,
trapped in a magnificent, hopeless
affair. He loved her — compromised her — but
she was already married; when they parted,
her husband burned their love-nest to the ground.

That night, I dreamed of slender yellow fingers
writhing from the tops of trees, and curls
of silver smoke gauzing the hedges. Walls
on four sides reddened, heaved and buckled
while a great wind howled across the bed.

Then quietly, the lavender of morning
spilled over me; I touched the sleeping man
beside me, and the cool sheet on my skin
was light, serene — utterly unlike the raw,
tumultuous world of wild longing, of flame.

Lady Hamilton's Portrait

National Maritime Museum, Greenwich

And now that the chromosomes have quit
their dance, and the silt of centuries
has sifted through the blue plasm
to settle on the bottom in cryptic rows,
I see you've come back, Emma Hamilton —

the curve of your cheek having bobbed
to the surface like a jettisoned peach,
the flesh prevailing over warp
and weft of canvas, the eyes
black as standing water.

I see you lifting your fingers
in their circlets of gold, waving
glittering arcs to loitering sailors
as if it were once again Horatio, Horatio
triumphant, coming to claim you, to sweep you home.

From your weighty golden frame, Emma Hamilton,
could you have predicted squalor? or that
your ripe lip, feathering, would tremble,
flaking cadmium yellow and red
on the ormolu sand?

The Odalisques

*Images beamed to Earth from the Voyager 2
spacecraft reveal that the moons of Uranus
feature topographical oddities both baffling
and bizarre.*

— *News item*

Here they come, the tiny tattered moons
of Uranus, their fluttering black chaddors
still shrouding them, from the farthest rooms
of interplanetary space. The scars

of ancient fires are frozen on their faces —
faces ravaged by the labyrinth
of ragged rings and elemental gases
reeling above their icebound planet-prince.

Delivered now from their hermetic cells,
these elfin freaks — wounded and mortified —
permit us to draw back their heavy veils
and hear their frenzied whispers from the void.

Earth Mother

Year after year your garden
burgeoned with more children,
some gathered in your lap,
some spilling from your skirts, half-ripe.

But not now, not anymore;
it's time to shut down. You have worn
the place out (too many tenants)
and now you have a thistle growing in it

that must be plucked. Flower, stem, and shoots,
it must be plucked — pulled out by the roots.
And down in the gully where your rare
garden grew, there will be a cavern, bare

and smooth; where if your hand should press
down on that emptiness, it will find no trace
of life; except for regular cascades
of pain, as if the knife were still inside.

No Two Exactly Alike

Why have you closed yourself upstairs for hours
tending to a poem on this icy-moist, keen
April day? You and I could be outdoors
walking the woods, our boots leaving wet green
stains between the snowdrops and the paper-whites
still buried to their chins in snow, but no,
you've drifted up the stairs again to write
down still another simile for snow.

A Love Song, Continued

What do you mean, going gray
like that — letting thin air
cross-hatch your face with lines
from some old poem I don't
care to read?

Come, get up! Take off
your heavy hat
your narrow shoes
and chase me, shouting,
to the waterside.

Two floats will be waiting there,
one glazed and wet, the other
powdered with pale sand.
Climb on — we'll paddle
with our hands

steering into coves canopied
with oleander and rowdy spills
of lantana; bright hair streaming,
we will storm the beaches
on our strong legs.

Later, half asleep and glutted
with sun, we will hold
one another, thigh
to reddened thigh, gritty,
languorous, gilded with the sea

and we'll ride on swells
of blue infinity —
you out front,
and me a starfish
clinging to your foot.

The Nanny

Mademoiselle ascends the stairs
to gather my baby into her strong arms
and sing to him her high *chansons,*
   to surender a finger to his grip
   tight as a lover's.

I watch her anoint his marbled skin
with bathwater, cushioning
in the crook of her arm
   his tufted head
   so loosely attached.

She nods to me: *Go out, Madame,*
go dancing, make a night of it!
but the music plucks
   at the hem of my skirt
   tugging me home.

Now from behind the door
I hear them crooning
together in the sultry dark,
   Gallic vowels purring
   in his throat.

Outside the Frame

Outside the Frame:
the Photographer's Last Letters to her Son

I.

Wildwood Farm, VT,:

April 3, 1991

Dear Chipper,
        Well, it's starting over — April's
back debauching us again, the woods
are soaking wet, the mud dazzles, all
our stringy willow trees are going blond
and sentimental (just like the women
who write about them) — and I rise to the sight
of the grass nudging up green, brimming
with narcissi, practically overnight!
— Narcissi. From a distance, don't they look
like froth? Or whitecaps? Makes me want to run
away to sea — *my* sea, Chip. A maverick
ocean that doesn't move, but invites me in
to take its photograph, to document
its miracles. So this morning, in I went . . .

April 20, 1991

It's my seventy-fifth April (sixty-fourth
with a camera in my hand) . . . and you wonder
why I desert my comfortable hearth
to crouch down on a patch of soggy tundra
taking pictures in the cold. Well, I'll

tell you why: it's to press my hands
against that rough young grass, to feel it yield
under my fingers, then to turn my lens
on the wetness underneath, where the soil
hides its buried treasure. Granite pearls,
flint sequins, limestone underpinnings — they're all
uncovered now, everthing's exposed! The voyeur
in me goes feverish inside my head
watching seeds moving in their satin bed.

April 29, 1991

. . . I'm cold today, Chipper. My jeans have two
black ovals in the front from where I knelt
to watch the moss, and it was well past noon
before I gave it up. (Everyone thought
I'd stayed too long; guess I'm getting old
and strange . . . .) But where was I? Mice? No, moss.
The farmers used to call it "elfin gold"
because it only grows in crevices
and caves. It doesn't want the sun at all —
just what the sun leaves behind, the dwindling
evidence of light — something like the pall
that hovers around a burnt-out candle.
They found me humming, reading with my thumb
its little poem to the millennium . . .

II.

Massachusetts General Hospital:

May 22, 1991

In response to your rude questions on the state
of my health: I am of sound mind

and in my hands I hold the weight
of my soul, a leaden comfort

in my palm. Its polished crystal eye
open, finds, fixes on the edges

of the enemy: a wall of grass,
leaves, stalks and stems, tapestries

of roots and vines — the wild green Other
that follows me, no matter how

I slash and scythe my little path —
pursues me, even as I back away . . .

III.

Wildwood Farm:

October 2, 1991

I must compose
myself, Chipper
and admit to you
that I am terribly
frightened, the camera
has developed so many
numbers and dials
I forget what they
mean; its rings
and buttons are all
mixed up and when
I finally try
to take a picture all
I see is parts
of my own eye
bristling with
daggers, staring
back at me
grotesque and huge

I must compose
and focus the lens
for precise pinpoint
focusing I must turn
the focusing ring until
the shimmering image
becomes sharp I must
use fast shutter speeds
to stop action stop
action or I will produce
a deliberate blur except
for certain unusual
lighting situations when
I must use the exposure
compensation dial to prevent
over-exposure I must
turn and turn until
the split image
becomes whole

IV.

Wildwood Farm:

January 25, 1992

Obviously the FBI
has come to find hard
evidence of my
incompetence. They
think they're fooling me,
they even say I
have met them before,
but I have never
met them before, these
blond harpies who keep
asking me my name
and what day it is
today (Up Yours-day?)
and the exact where-
abouts of my gloves
and earmuffs,
the pinking shears,
the keys to the
boathouse, my Knirps
umbrella (as if I
needed it in winter!)
the pancake syrup,
the bottle of
cocktail onions,
the thumbtacks, the
remote-control
TV channel changer,
extra extra pink
Pepto-Bismol,

some kitchen
safety matches
and a couple
of bowls of
excellent vanilla
custard from
Christmas.

V.

The Roundtree Convalescent Home:

February 4, 1992

. . . whereas now I hold my hands
at arms length and point
my index fingers skyward
and extend my thumbs
so that they meet tip to tip
thus making a frame (minus the top)

and with my frame I scan
the scenery; here a clump
of white buildings,
there a face, or a flower,
but so often nothing, Chip —
nothing at all

VI.

Roundtree:

February 14, 1992

The loud-talking
women are back
with their folding

table and their
jigsaw puzzle:
"A Yorkshire Dale"

showing part of
a hill and some
trees with huge holes

in them as if
a cannonball
had torn through their

upper reaches.
Try, the women
yell, to find the

pieces, look, here
is some sky! But
it's hard, because

many are lost;
some are under
the table or

buried in the
cushions, a few
have been purloined —

23

slipped into the
untied bathrobe
of a hairless

geezer who says
he knows just where
the big tower

went, meanwhile in
our ears someone
croons Would we like

to swing on a
star? and at last
they wheel away

the puzzle and
bring another
in, dumping it

out and smiling —
as if to say
Maybe you won

that round, grandmaw,
but it's just a
matter of time.

VII.

Roundtree:

March 11, 1992

All I know is that it's
about this big
and I need it for
the things I do but
I can't remember
what it's called. You put it
in the bigger thing
and it keeps it there
for you so when you want
to look at something later
there it is.
You know what I mean,
it's about so big
and it's not square, it
isn't square at all,
it's that other.
You have to use it
to make things stay where
they used to be
so you can take them out
and look at them where they were.
But God help me I
can't find it anywhere.
All I know for certain
is that it's about this big
and I need it, I need it very much.

VIII.

Massachusetts General Hospital :

March 30, 1992

Have you come to say hello
maybe you will take me
I think it must be time
time to go now
goodbye

IX.

Wildwood Farm

April?

There are times each day
when I go   off
                                                    somewhere

when I return there is a little less of me
        as if

            each time   mind and
                        one thread of memory

                                        were pulled away

                    become
Soon I shall be
                    entirely
                        unravelled

26

I shall survive

             as
                  ** *afterimage* **
             as
                  ** *gatherer of light* **

Legacies

The Boy on the Plane

The boy on the plane is coming home
from his grandfather's funeral — his first
exposure to the way it's done, how we comb
and scrub and manicure and dress
the body, wiping away the evidence
of life's final squalor. He stares into his lap,
while a half-dream plays along his lips.

On either side of us, the clouds
are climbing into mounded, coalescing
heaps — how voluptuous they look, viewed from the side,
their secret folds and cumulations riding
on shafts of wild, sliding
air. Yawning enormously, the boy turns and smiles
with pleasure at the girl across the aisle.

I think about old men, and of the boy
beside me, how it's almost time
for him; and of the girl he will someday
press against in a cool, darkened room.
And the heaviness I've known
before, that profound wrenching I recognize
grinds forward, and settles into place.

Leaving the Peonies

Avoid thinking of them. Concentrate
instead on what we're loading in the van:
the wicker furniture, the silverplate,
the dogs, the parakeet, the IBM.
Don't dwell on the tangled tapestry
of roots wintering behind the evergreens,
or the sideshow they'll put on in May —
bursting into Harvest Moons, Doreens,
ten-inch Dinner Plates (*overweight shrub goes
Hollywood!*) — and that we won't be here
to see them. Foolish. Instead of peonies,
think high-rise, fresh paint, conditioned air —
   Who needs another torrid night that reeks
   of Carmine, Curlilocks, Angel Cheeks?

Message from the Ice Cave

For Rachel, after the death
of her young daughter.

I am living here now, where the cold
is my consort, the lover I clasp
with my arms and legs, from whose gray
blanket I tear each breath.

All around me ice is in bloom —
tiny glass buds keep swelling
from hairline fissures
in the stone. The buried river

cuts close, a dark ventricle
thick with sorrow. Moisture floods
my face, pools at my feet.
In time, a tower of ice

will grow around me, taking
the shape of an old woman
and visitors will say, Look at her,
how she weeps into her hands.

Conundrum

She cannot fathom what God had in mind
or what eternal Truth was brought to bear
when Beethoven went deaf, and Milton blind.

Although she knows God will be disinclined
to answer her subversive little prayer,
she cannot fathom what He had in mind.

How many masterworks were left behind —
unwritten verses, music lost in air —
when Beethoven went deaf, and Milton blind?

Was God afraid of being undermined
by feats as near to the sublime as theirs?
If not, she can't tell what He had in mind

unless He was incensed with humankind,
flinging back to Earth His own despair
when Beethoven went deaf, and Milton blind.

How will she bear it, should she find
no other answer but that God could err —
and who can tell her what He had in mind
when Beethoven went deaf, and Milton blind?

One Last Favor

Why yes,
there is something
you can do for us
before you die.
You can please quit
grieving. Stop

leaking out all over us
the horror and the
dread. It's hard
for us to watch,
we don't like it,

we would so much rather
have you smiling like
a picture of Saint Jude,
stroking our hands and
telling us There there,

this was to be expected.
But with your whole spine
gone bent like that and
your head shaking back
and forth, your eyelids

stiff with fear and every
wasted muscle straining
to deny, deny — just where
are we supposed to turn
for comfort now?

Piano Overture

He came to our apartment twice a year
to tune my mother's piano. All day long
we tiptoed, trying not to interfere
with what to us were strange, unearthly songs.

He never struck a heavy, luscious chord —
only fifths, fourths, octaves — clean and spare;
brandishing his hammer like a sword,
we watched him wring concordance from the air.

Taut as pulled wire, he'd lean into the keys,
his practiced fingers pressing note on note,
hunting down aberrant harmonies
and any latent quaver in the throat.

At last the piano, gaping and undone,
its very heart exposed for all to see,
would wait in silence, chastened as a nun,
for the blasphemies of Chopin and Satie.

The Vow

I mustn't ever have another drink.
I'm stronger than I've ever been before,
and this time it's going to work, I think.

Still, I know you'd raise a holy stink
if I should come careening through that door
saying I'll never have another drink.

You'd tell me to go and see a shrink
or call the idiot marriage counselor.
But this time it's going to work. I think

the kids would be surprised — they'd blink
like I was going to fall down on the floor,
but I would not have had a single drink

and they'd see how far I've come from the brink
of disaster. So don't worry anymore,
not this time. It's going to work, and I think

you should consider letting me link
up with you again — because I swore
last night I'd never have another drink,
and this time it's going to work. I think.

Speculations While Walking Through Lake Park Without My Dog

For Gopher, 1979-1992

-1-

If suddenly the world were recalibrated
and all the dogs in it would age
just one year
to our quick seven,
we would begin by laying plans
for the century ahead:

-2-

Gazing into cups of dark tea,
sons and daughters would murmur
long into the night about the spaniel
they have taken in. Uneasy,
tilting forward in their chairs,
they would talk about the future,
their unborn heirs — those pale
peevish ghosts, will they welcome this?
Will they suffer a spayed bitch at midlife,
energy dwindling, dewlaps trembling,
rollicking hips stiffening
with displasia?

Lord, are we ungenerous
in handing down to them what
they must love?

3

Consider this: a golden retriever
vaulting the chainlink for three generations
of kids careening home from school. Already
legend would have cited him
for clothesline larceny,
tennis ball abuse, and harassment
of a coloratura fieldmouse that squealed
till it swooned

but if you followed this very dog
to the bedside of a dying woman,
you might have seen her fingering his ear,
whispering *You remember Emily
from when she was little, don't you, boy?*
whereupon he would sigh (as dogs do)
and blink benignly at the white azaleas
massed and wilting on the sill.

You're our dog now, pronounces great-granddaughter,
leading the graying airedale to the bowl
of warm milk. She will be the last
to care for him, having missed altogether
the eager elbows and giddy tongue
of the early decades,
inheriting instead the cloudy eye,
the failing kidney,
the longest ride.

A dog's death demands much pomp —
old tags and artifacts
must be carefully arranged,
scrapbooks dusted, propped,
cracked open to the light

where here, across the stiff manila pages
an incessant puppy races
with the fast-growing pines —
and there, a long and gorgeous prime
romps with the shadows of vanished children

until at last, old age nudges up
against the hand — hinting
at a growing drowse, a grand inclination
to bed down in the perennials
of a hundred summers.

In Lake Park this morning,
the cold air leaps
with calls and whistles from the frozen field

while my memory —
a creature of habit —
circles three more times around Gopher's grave.

Caveat for Poets

Never, never write of war
from your soft bed on the second floor.

Don't discuss the recent slaughter
as you sip French mineral water

and spare the world your villanelle
that bleats and re-bleats *war is hell.*

We know, without your telling us
that guns are awfully dangerous;

and we'll be glad to verify
that some get hurt, and some will die.

In fact, it looks like you've decided
the whole damn business is misguided —

war seems such a bad mistake,
and violence makes your temples ache —

so let's pretend you've had your say.
We quite agree. Now go away.

Tercets from the Train

Human dramas implode without trace.

— Marge Piercy

Gorgeous, they are gorgeous, these two women getting
    on the train, one in lime green silk, black hair
      a mile wide, the other slim as a whip, coiled

in red linen. Their two small boys, grinning,
    have squirmed into facing seats, bubbling with spare
      energy, the cuffs of their designer jeanlets rolled

at the ankles, their studded shirts glinting.
    I overhear the women talking over what to wear
      to some convention (should it be the gold

Armani or the St. Laurent?) while the boys are gazing
    through the rain-spattered window, practicing their
      locomotive lingo in shrill, five-year-old

voices, demanding information: are we going
    faster than a plane, where is the engineer,
      does this train have electricity or coal?

But the women's eyes are fierce, they are grumbling
    over Lord & Taylor, which was once a store
      to be reckoned with, although the one with wild

hair points out that even Bloomingdale's is growing
    more K-Martish than it ever was before.
      Don't you interrupt me, child,

she hisses to the boy who wonders why the train is grinding
so slowly through the towns, and where
the bathroom is and what the ticket-man is called

until she bends over him, glaring
from beneath her shadowed eyes, a crimson flare
on either cheek. *You're interrupting me,* she growls.

Now you'll be sorry. His mouth is gaping
as the flat of her hand splits the air,
annihilating two long rows of smiles.

I warned you, didn't I, darling?
Now don't you dare cry. Don't you dare.
Up and down the aisle, the silence howls.

Notes from a Family Picnic

Life hasn't been easy for Betsy since she turned
thirteen — just look at her, the sniffy way
she sits all by herself, wincing with scorn
at her noisy cousins lining up to play
a pick-up softball game before the day
runs out. *Childish*, she mutters from the chair
in which she lounges, tossing back her hair.

But now, two uncles and a favorite aunt
are filling in at right field and third base;
Betsy's breathing quickens, but she can't
stop buffing her nails, sucking in her face,
keeping her careful distance — just in case
we take her for that splendid child *Betsy*
who left us only recently.

To My Neighbor John, Who Is Completely Happy

That midnight warble in the summer dark
is you, John, singing your way home
from the Rehab Center where you work
evenings — one out-of-kilter chromosome
has never slowed you down. Your nightly whoop
floods the neighborhood with so much bliss
that my Dalmatian springs from sleep
and opens up her throat to harmonize
with you — along with every other canine
in a one-mile radius. Soon the air
is vibrating for blocks with strains
of an unearthly sweetness — prayers
rising from the bottom of the brain,
an ode to joy, with tabernacle choir.

Interludes

In Tanzania

Tonight I sleep
with the grass-eaters:
zebra and wildebeest
doze in clusters
near my tent, as night
gathers in pools
over the high savannah.

Even under canvas I
am caught in a current
of dread as it eddies
past, ruffling mane
and beard. My herd
shudders as if one
creature, and listens.

Now the deep African sky
lifts a glittering claw;
we, the vulnerable, hear
the rasp of death
and twitch our haunches
as the golden cat
begins her dance.

Late in the Wet Season

when field grass is strung with gold from blade
to blade, the gazelles
come in herds, to graze.
The nursing mothers cluster
at the peripheries,
while their leggy newborns learn
to stand breathless
at the least flutter of danger.

Muzzily drunk on rare vapors
rising from the soil,
one fawn sends its own sweet redolence
out on the wind. Soon
the lion comes for the kill, closing
the space between them — their forms
link, they churn
the high grass.

Later, one by one, the others stumble
from their hideouts, each looking
for the familiar flank, the bulwark, the fortress
in the golden grass.
And a lone doe shakes her head (as if
clearing her memory)
before turning to the herd again,
to be of the herd, to graze
and graze.

The Globetrotter

He had been almost everywhere — Acapulco, Venice,
Pebble Beach, the south of France, Grenada
long before that absurd war. And now he craved
the glamour of East Africa — fabled Kenya,
wrinkled khaki, William Holden, all
that. He took a week's accommodation
at the same timbered, sprawling old hotel
where Hemingway himself had had occasion
to roister, it was claimed, where the great
white drinkers of endangered cognacs still came
to talk safari. Ecstatic on his first night,
he slept till nearly noon in his room's
deep twilight, languidly waking to confront
the middle of the day. With American Express
pressed to his heart, he prepared for hunting
down the proper khaki shorts and many-pocketed vests
and maybe one of those splendid round hats.
But first, breakfast (French toast, Dutch pastry)
in the curtained coffee shop — then out,
out the glass doors and into the blazing,
no, the blinding frieze of white light, but with black
shapes pelting past flashing orange, green
and yellow-green, and black, purple and flaming pink
and black, especially black, no khaki to be seen,
almost dancing, somehow, with their arms wide
and hands flying free and jabbering in Swahili
jambo, jambo! Aghast, he stumbled back inside,
    reeling.
                    And when the steward on the plane
asked him what he thought of Africa, he said, Christ,
I never saw so goddamn many Africans,
and pressed his fingertips against his eyes.

Lost Lines from Whitby Abbey

670 A.D.

Late last evening   a layman of Whitby,
a man admired   for his modest demeanor

and kindly way   with the cattle and swine,
gave us a song   in a grievous soprano,

in a voice that could wither   the vine from the wall.
We turned away   and tried to look solemn

but soon we were laughing   and some so loudly,
the clamor was heard   in cloister and chancel.

Then one of our number   waved his hand
and we paused to listen   to this laborer's song;

we began to hear   his hoarse re-telling
of the age-old tale   of the earth's beginnings.

Its wisdom seared   the souls of the brethren,
its music clasped us   closer to God;

we shut our eyes   in sheer stupefaction,
scarcely believing   the scope of our fortune —

the song of the Lord   was sweeter than milk
on the rough tongue   of this rustic farmer.

Today we will take him   by his time-worn hand
all ruddy and knobbed   from the rake and the hoe

and beg him to sit   on a bench of smooth stone
and sing once again   of the grace of the Father.

We shall cluster about him   with quills in our fingers
scratching his verses   on scrolls of fine vellum —

for here in the gloom   of this gray outpost Whitby
slammed by black waves   and salt-soaked wind,

in this wild country   where kings and demi-kings
ride to their destinies   deep in the sod,

where the dales to the south   all die into moors,
where ghosts and devils   dance for the Godless —

here, here is the place   that our heavenly Lord
sent to us Caedmon,   where Caedmon sings.

I Know a Bank
Where the Wild Thyme Blows

Judy I still
remember how we
would sometimes drive
through the arboretum
on our way
to the Park Street
A & W for root
beer floats (Too
much, we'd have decided
in the car, too much
Milton, too much Spenser,
Donne and Shakespeare)
and how we slowed beside
a stand of lilac trees
posturing in pale blue
and laced with drowsy musk,
beckoning with fingers
dripping petals;
and how we ran to them,
our summer dresses lifting,
bare arms raised, our hair
gilded with pollen as we
assumed our places, mimicking
the age-old choreography
turn for turn, dip for
dip, enchanted
as Titania,
insatiable
as Mab.

Mammography

It's a human trait, this odd compulsion
to burrow under every surface
looking for what can't be seen — buried treasure,
captive pearl, and now this sacred scarab,

furtive and dangerous in its velvet sac
of blood and tissue, carried near the heart.
It brings with it an ancient curse, a black
commandment: whoever owns it has to part

her gown and lean against a pale window
while a dozen dawns fluoresce and flicker,
then a shadow comes — spreading, unwelcome
as a thumbprint — darkening the lower

quadrant of this most tender place
on the woman with the ashen face.

What They Don't Know

They are thirteen, all flying elbows
and thinbone knees, wrapping their tongues
around words like *pimp* and *bare-ass*
and *hard-on.* They are astounded
by girls, the bodies of girls, the onrush
of skin and hair, and they talk about
what it would be to touch one of those
flashy breasts, to look it in the eye.

They are thirteen, and they don't know
about the Buick they might be riding in
a year or two from now, packed in hip-to-hip
chanting a frenzied *go   go   go   go*
until the pavement starts to bulge
and crest, lifting them, sending them up
into some kind of heartstop heaven.

They don't know that the tree might be an elm
that the car will wrap itself around
in lascivious embrace, or that afterwards
a thin, watery sigh   *Open the door*
could be the first sound and the last
before sirens take up the threnody.

For now, though, they lean lightly
on their slender bikes, polishing
a new language: *horny, piss-off, kiss my ass.*
Expertly they palm their cigarettes,
the thick smoke streaming
from their mouths and noses.

Miss Martin at Four O'Clock

I am LaShanda's teacher
and to LaShanda that is all
I am. Every day she waits
for this, the breakaway hour
when the windows of my eyes
start to blacken behind
the neat rows of paper cutouts
facing the street
and the wide broom of darkness
comes, pushing blood-red
dust along my corridors.

LaShanda thinks I sleep
in a wooden drawer, folded
on a bed of thumbtacks — my
left hand gripping a bone
of chalk that screams
by day, while my right
brandishes a scarlet
Eversharp, scattering
the swarm of butterflies
that will drift forever
in LaShanda's head.

Drive All Night

Simply set your cruising speed at sixty-eight,
stick to the Interstate, and you'll arrive
like morning's minion, pal — your hair
wind-flattened on one side, pulse walloping
at optimum efficiency, tight schedule intact.
Just repeat after me: *avoid small towns.*

That's right, eschew those towns,
friend, those glomerations of eight
or nine hundred rubes named Dwayne, intact
in their dullness. Their collective aim: to arrive
at the local wienie-works on time — hair
greased, molars brushed, haunches walloping.

It's true, of course, that your own walloping
windshield wipers could turn some of these towns
(for all their Wal-Marts and parking meters and Hair
Chalets) into vapor-lit versions of eight-
eenth century streetscapes. Especially if you arrive
under canopies of ancient elms, all intact.

And if a row of bungalows, equally intact,
happens to feature one lace curtain walloping
crazily in the night breeze, you might arrive
at certain conclusions about small towns.
You might even come within a hair
of staying for supper. Even if you just ate.

Maybe you find a chrome diner, circa 1958,
with pictures of Charlie Chaplin tacked
to the walls. A waitress with long copper hair
grins and takes your order: a walloping
plate of beans and ham, followed by the town's
finest apple pie. The locals start to arrive:

> *Where's your girl, Dwayne? You got a riv-*
> *al, buddy? You just been eight-*
> *balled? Well, here's what the town's*
> *been saying — she ain't what you call intact,*
> *boy. Broad needs a good walloping*
> *to keep her zipped up and out of your hair.*

— Fade out. No diner, no copper hair, no small towns.
Only those walloping tires and the hum of your V-8.
Drive all night, friend. Arrive intact.

The Showdown

Okay, Zucchini,
with your sleek Sicilian good looks —
I know all about you and the rest
of the zucca family, how you start out
small, in a corner of some
respectable old *giardino* (nobody
even notices) and then you spread,
don't you, till you've moved in on
all the little guys, the beans
and the carrots and cukes,
and pretty soon you're in charge
of the whole damn *fattoria*, right?
Well, I've got news for you, pal,
you're past your prime. You're ripe
to spend the rest of your natural
life in the cooler. Think I'm kidding?
Listen, either play along or it's
    Ratatouille!   Ratatouille!
— a year in the jug for you, Zuke.
And your little tomato, too.

Memorabilia

The Art Student

There on her paper
the silhouette of a ginkgo
resembled the outline of a mushroom cloud

as a certain warp
in visual acuity
took over: some optical skullduggery

trapping images
on their unsuspecting journey
to the brain, subjecting them to measures of

skillful retouching
before releasing them — skewed —
yet quite capable of long-term survival.

Before You Were Born

your shadow trailed
plumes of helium;

you sang atomic
madrigals in high

carbonic whispers;
from your harp came all

the scales and measures
of plane geometry

ten thousand suns
burst vermillion

through the silken sutures
holding night to day;

flexing, transparent,
thin as a disc

you skimmed the hummocks
of galactic dust

spaceflowers
bloomed in your blood

light-years tethered your
root to your seed

and you slept, folded
between billows

dreaming strange phantasms
of onyx

mica, flint
and bone.

The Mysterious Collection of the Capuchin Monks

The most uncelebrated church in Rome
is deeply pocked and overrun with stone
cancer (the buses spit grime

waist-high); and in its dim entryway
an old disheveled monk thumbs his dirty
coinpurse, hoping you'll stop by.

He says he's got something to show
you — *magnifico*, he whispers, winking, as though
you and he were sharing secrets. So you go

with him, down forty, fifty stairs. The light
is dim; the air thick and cold, fraught
with exhalations from an era not

your own. Then he raises his hand
and points to a row of glowing doorways behind
you, saying, *Ecco, ecco!* so you'll understand

to look in every room. And there they are: The bones.
The clavicles, the vertebrae, the skulls, the skeletons —
palisades of bones, all arranged in murals and designs.

Some could well be chicken bones, gray and flecked
around a crucifix, but most are pink
or faintly blue and iridescent, worked

intricately into flower shapes on lattices of rib.
Still others — rounded pelvises, smooth ilium
rosettes — garnish every altarstone and crypt.

Mother of God, you think, they saved these bones
and fashioned pretty pictures out of bones,
and people come to marvel at the bones —

You turn and face the little man in brown
who stands aside, all bones himself, eyes cast down —
and something shudders, deep inside your own.

At Pompano

Mrs. Sugarman walks the beach
swatting at cans with her aluminum cane,
stepping over blankets paved with rich
Cubanos playing cards, picking her way between
long rows of rumps, parallel parked, aglint with oil.

She knows of a shore where the sand
spreads cold in the shade — where pebbles
cling like crumbs to a foamy lip of land —
and where the sun, blistered and feeble,
exerts itself for such a little while

that it's still August when the draped clouds come,
and soon what has to die will die. But here
at Pompano, the summer dodders on,
redolent and rotting, spilling itself tier on tier
over this hot graveyard, this torrid funeral.

Speak to Me in the Oldest Tongue

and let me hear
the rugged consonants
rattling their percussion down
the centuries; and vowels
like reeds, set shimmering by
an eloquent intake of breath
six thousand years ago and still
pulsing, having cleaved
into hundred-part harmony;

sing for me
the trills of southern Spain,
the arpeggios of Tuscany,
the thick, moist velars
of the Schwarzwald; strike the
alto bells of India and
the cymbals of Kildare — each a
variation on an ancient air,
the plainsong of angels.

Some Urgent Questions for the Peasant Woman
in the National Geographic Magazine

1.
How old are you, *grandmere*?

2.
At what moment did you opt for being ancient,
for hunching your bright shoulders
into that rusty sack,
your fierce hair trussed and hung to cure
beneath your kerchief?

3.
Did you hurl straight from youth
to cronehood, or was there a brief housewifely
interval between?

4.
Important: How did you decide
that it was time?

5.
Have you daughters, madame?

6.
Do they think your face
looks like a Provencal tartuffe?

7.

Do they speed away
in sports cars, laughing (as your teeth
drop one by one from your mouth)?

8.

Or do they endure under aprons,
slinging babies from hip to shoulder, squinting
at the sun, laying plans for covering their hair?

Free Lunch

They are known as urban deer.
Their address is the nature
preserve where
they are stalked
by flocks of weekend naturalists.

But we who live nearby know
how deer will come calling where
food blooms in
little rows —
convenient, and so enticing that

in spite of all the fanfare
from overwrought carnivores
with names like
Bojangles,
garden becomes cafeteria.

Urban deer seem unaware
that we had no intention
of planting
seventeen
tea roses just to satisfy their

penchant for leafy greens, but
try explaining that to the
customers.
So we sigh
and continue to work their tables.

Report from the Outpost

Hannah pasted stars
on her ceiling

and every night
from a galaxy

never mapped
by any astronomer,

a greenish glow
lights the frozen faces

of a colony
of stuffed animals.

Cecily

She was a poet, and had a poet's face —
    a nimble and unruly face
        that danced to the metrics

in her head. Verses, to her,
    sprouted at every open window;
        just the slightest

readjustment of the lines
    at the corners of her eyes
        could make them bloom.

Her kitchen table — an arsenal
    of spaceships, popguns, Cheerios —
        was her seat of inspiration. There

she would mold a prosody for what she saw:
    kids in raincoats, two survivor elms, jonquils
        shattered by frost

that crazy year when all the gardens froze
    to death in June
        and winter never really ended.

Of all her poems, I remember
    that one best — the verbs pelted,
        nouns piled up in drifts;

when it appeared in print
    she had the neighbors over
        for coffee and champagne.

The hot blind pain amazed her.
  It started as a trickle
    deep in the chest, then

hardened to a red bullet on
  a vascular trajectory, lodging
    at a point behind her eye.

At the hospital
  it welled and burst
    before they got it out.

Last year they told us she
  has finally stopped rocking
    and thumping out unheard-of rhythms
  in her chair, and can manage
in the bathroom by herself.

Sparrow Invades University Library

On winter's darkest afternoon
a bird, bitten with cold, pushed through the crack
between the downspout and the frozen brick,
    and found encapsulated June.

In her rapture, she mistook
the glare for sun, the stacks for vegetation,
and — stunned by her miraculous migration —
    turned for sustenance to books.

State Line

Every time the family drove down
to Chicago, Dad would point to the same
stone farmhouse, saying if I spent
the night there, one side
of my bed would be in Wis-

consin, the other in Illinois.
And from deep in the back seat I would hear
the throb of Wabash Avenue
and the caterwaul
of elevated trains in

my right ear, and in my left, the hushed
percussion of a dozen blue mallards,
rising like a great flapping sail
from the surface of
a sandy-bottomed lake.

In the Midnight Cupboard

      white flour is moving, alive
with silent implosions
    of wormlife. Prodded by
       dim congenital memories,
these protomoths
    curl upward to find

     the dark, to fuse
themselves to any indentation
    (chipped dish,
     lid without pot,
dimpled can)
    so each may grow

     the gray bubble
it will wear while
    dropping
      its shriveled mantle
of wormhood down
    over powdery, dun-colored

    wings.
Inevitably, when
    the doors fly open,
     a new generation
will burst blind
    into a horror of light.

Last Flight

My cat, who worships me, brought me a bird
and dropped it neatly, unobtrusively
on my doormat, where it greeted me
at six a.m., adroitly massacred.

A case, I thought, of true love run amok:
the corpse had been an adolescent finch
who, on a short foray from nest to branch
became not so much finch as sitting duck.

And now the scrawny victim lay in state
across my dustpan; I transported him
gently, acknowledging his martyrdom,
to the vacant lot across the street.

Thinking of it as his last flight, I hurled
him high into the sun, where he glittered
for a moment, airborne — then plunged, shattering
leaves, piercing all the morning's gold.

Memo to a Late Baby

Unlikely is
the word for you,

my young sprig, clear
winner in the old

game of dwindling
probabilities. You

never minded the
incipient jowls flap-

ping over your crib,
nor have you remarked

upon your enormous
cousins who drive

cars. Benignly you
settle for a slower

but steadier lope
through childhood,

as we (cheering
ourselves on)

head into extra innings.

Eventualities

Notice from the Sweet Chariot Funeral Parlor

> *Due to predicted overcrowding in our*
> *cemeteries, a new service is available*
> *which will see to packing and storing*
> *one's remains in a space capsule for*
> *eventual launching into Earth's orbit.*
>
> — *Discover Magazine*

Dear Friend, we
are operating at capacity
    and cannot
supply a green and grassy spot
    for your tomb,
as there is no more room.

Instead, you are invited to entrust
    your dust
to our space-age morticians, who seal
    in stainless steel
(thanks to post-Newtonian science)
    our clients.

Whereupon you
(and all your shiny loved ones, too)
    shall ascend
via chartered rocketship, to spend
    eternity
very near where Heaven used to be.

The Day After I Die

they will find the cure
for whatever got me,
and a unified theory
of physics will be announced
by a consortium
from M.I.T.

Following the funeral,
Earth will be contacted
by intelligent beings from
the Farquhar galaxy —
immediately after which
Chrysler will introduce a car
that can run forever
on table scraps.

Within the week,
Abbott Labs will introduce
an age-reversing cream
on the very heels of
a morning-after diet pill
that tastes like a Cadbury's
Easter Egg.

Finally,
the woman that they hire
to clean and fumigate my house
will come across a pile
of my old poems

and turn them over to
her Thursday client, Galway Kinnell,
who will gallantly take charge
and see to everything —
including, of course,
any immortality.

Space Invaders

Sometimes her back door opens
on a fleet of little crystal spheres

cruising past the power lines
and landing like an alien armada

in the grass. Clear
as water, weightless,

they shudder and withdraw
from her extended hand

and start exploding out
of their shimmering skins

before she has a chance
to shade her eyes —

each one releasing
into the placid afternoon

a throb of memory, stolen
from a world she has forgotten.

A few are trailing filaments
of time and place, guy-wires

to a partial vision: the crimson
smile, for instance, of a girl

in a straw hat — moon-beautiful,
stone-dead for years —

or a dim, dopplered voice
thick with armagnac and lust.

But the rest all fly apart,
with nothing to show

for their gyrotechnics
but a riffle of scent,

a small convulsion of bells,
a paralyzing entropy of light.

From a Dark Place

For A.E.L. (d.1974) and R.R.T. (b.1975)

Who are you, child, still floating
in my daughter's womb? I didn't know you
in my time, yet you look like me —
there is a flare to the nostril and a crimp
to the hair that is ours.

Your eyes are sealed like mine,
but your mouth opens and closes
with incipient messages —
if I should whisper back
you would listen, spinning with delight.

Unfold your fingers, if you can —
they are waiting to grow eloquent
and strong. They will move under mine
the first time you touch the watered silk
of an iris, or your mother's face.

Your bed narrows, your bones
are bonding as mine fall
to powder. Soon we will glide away
from one another — you won't remember
meeting me in the dissolving dark.

But you have my gifts:
the chromata of our past, strung jewels
I harbored for you all my life.
Without their weight, I vanish
just as you — moondrenched and beautiful — appear.

Sixty-Five

Stockbroker, accountant, tax attorney, Gas
Company vice-president, lift a brimming glass
to your moist-eyed colleague, whose turn it is
to be led by pinstripe underlings down from his
panelled chamber on Twelve, where the throne
has been shoved from the desk and the telephone
number changed. Tonight his picture graces
the long wall lined with dead men's faces.

The Tenth Avenue Care Home

If you're not ready for a nursing home,
live where you belong — in a beautiful
house in a pleasant neighborhood.

— the Yellow Pages

We live in this house.
It fits right in.
Its windows face
the long afternoons.

It fits right in,
and no one would guess
the long afternoons
mean nothing to us

and no one would guess
that the other houses
mean nothing to us —
except for the little boys

that the other houses
gather in at dusk.
The little boys
think we're ghosts,

gathering at dusk
to frequent their dreams.
they think we're ghosts
when our night visits seem

too frequent. Their dreams
make them shudder —
our night visits seem
like shadows, wavering but persistent.

Make them shutter
their windows, face
their own shadows. Wavering but persistent,
we live in this house.

At the End

In another time, a linen winding-sheet
would already have been drawn
about her; the funeral drums by now

would have throbbed their dull tattoo
into the shadows writhing
behind the fire's eye

while a likeness
of her narrow torso, carved
and studded with obsidian

might have been passed from hand
to hand and rubbed against the bellies
of women with child

and a twist of her gray hair
been dipped in oil
and set alight, releasing the essence

of her life's elixir, pricking
the nostrils of her children
and her children's children

whose amber faces nod and shine
like a ring of lanterns
strung around her final flare —

but instead, she lives in this white room
gnawing on a plastic bracelet
as she is emptied, filled, and emptied.

Golden Warriors End Year With Big Loss

Just look at you, doing the hangdog shuffle
back to the locker room, shoulder humps
bulging under your jersey like a couple
of wandering codpieces. You're in a slump,
all right — and someday it will dawn on you
that your hard body (even as we speak)
is already inching closer to
a long, inevitable losing streak —
and soon those hamstrung legs of yours will race
right past your final season, kiss of fame
and disillusion, years of commonplace
diversions. You're hurtling into overtime,
gaining yardage on your rocking chair,
your last pass, last play, last breath of air.

Clown

Watch.
I'm slipping into my old age.
A shabby get-up, full of holes,
it hangs from my shoulders
like a tattered old blanket.

I am a fright.
Ridiculous in these lumpy shoes —
see how my knees
poke out a wacky angles?
And look, my shins have gone
bird-thin under the veins.

Rose-red explosions
tattoo my thighs and rattle
the flesh along my arms;
even these bombshell breasts
deflate — surprise! —
and disappear.

My strings are loose.
My horns blow watery
and strange. The crowd titters
as I rise for my colossal pratfall
at the last possible second.